A
gift
honoring
Griffin
and
Carson
Gilchrist

Prickly PORCUPINES

GROSS-OUT DEFENSES

by Catherine Nichols

Consultant: Gabrielle Sachs
Zoo Educator

BEARPORT PUBLISHING

NEW YORK, NEW YORK

Credits

Cover and Title Page, © Bruce Corbett/Alamy; TOC, © Tasha Lavigne/Shutterstock; 4, © Ronald Toms/Oxford Scientific/Photolibrary; 5, © Thomas Kitchin & Victoria Hurst/kitchinhurst.com; 6, © Randy Brandon/AlaskaStock.com; 7, © Keith Douglas/All Canada Photos Inc./age fotostock; 8, © John Pitcher/Design Pics Inc./Alamy; 9, © Richard Kolar/Animals Animals-Earth Scenes; 10, © Daniel J Cox/Natural Exposures; 11, © Brian Colton; 12-13, © D.Robert Franz/ImageState/Alamy; 15, © Mary Ann McDonald/Corbis; 16, © Maresa Pryor/Animals Animals-Earth Scenes; 17, © Tom Brakefield/Corbis; 18, © R. Wittek/Arco Images/Peter Arnold Inc.; 19, © Stephen J. Krasemann/DRK Photo; 20, © Tim Fitzharris/Minden Pictures/Getty Images; 21, © Tom Brakefield/Getty Images; 22, © Carl Warner/Getty Images; 23TL, © Maresa Pryor/Animals Animals-Earth Scenes; 23TR, © Maresa Pryor/Animals Animals-Earth Scenes; 23BL, © Bev Wigney; 23BR, © Daniel J Cox/Natural Exposures.

Publisher: Kenn Goin
Senior Editor: Lisa Wiseman
Creative Director: Spencer Brinker
Design: Becky Munich
Photo Researcher: James O'Connor

Library of Congress Cataloging-in-Publication Data

Nichols, Catherine.
 Prickly porcupines / by Catherine Nichols.
    p. cm. — (Gross-out defenses)
 Includes bibliographical references and index.
 ISBN-13: 978-1-59716-721-5 (library binding)
 ISBN-10: 1-59716-721-5 (library binding)
 1. Porcupines—Juvenile literature. 2. Animal defenses—Juvenile literature. I. Title.

 QL737.R652N53 2009
 599.35'97—dc22

                              2008009369

For more information, write to Bearport Publishing Company, Inc., 101 Fifth Avenue, Suite 6R, New York, New York 10003. Printed in the United States of America.

10 9 8 7 6 5 4 3 2

Contents

Armed and Dangerous 4

Back Off! 6

A Spiky Tail. 8

Sharp and Deadly 10

Tiny Pincushions 12

Tree Houses 14

Tasty Trees 16

Living and Learning 18

A Long, Prickly Life 20

Another Prickly Defense 22

Glossary 23

Index 24

Read More 24

Learn More Online 24

About the Author 24

Armed and Dangerous

A hungry porcupine climbs a tree looking for a snack.

Out of nowhere a mountain lion appears.

Scared, the porcupine raises its sharp **quills**.

It swings its spiky tail and hits the lion.

Ouch! A bunch of quills stick in the lion's face.

Yelping in pain, the lion runs away.

A porcupine's coat is made up of long hairs and soft thick fur. It also contains about 30,000 prickly quills.

Back Off!

Before striking, a porcupine tries to scare an enemy away by using different tricks.

First, the porcupine turns its back to the enemy and raises its needle-sharp quills.

The longest, stiffest quills are on the prickly animal's back.

If that warning doesn't work, the porcupine clicks its top and bottom teeth together.

The scary sound tells the enemy to leave before it gets hurt.

teeth

Sometimes a porcupine makes a stinky smell when it's in danger. The horrible odor is so strong it can make an enemy's eyes and nose water. Phew!

A Spiky Tail

The prickly porcupine frightens away many enemies, but not all of them.

If an enemy comes too close after being warned, the porcupine attacks it.

While walking backward, the porcupine slaps the enemy with its strong, spiky tail.

The sharp quills come off easily and stab the enemy's skin.

Ouch!

Porcupines flick their tails so quickly that it can look as if the quills are flying through the air. However, porcupines aren't really shooting their quills.

tail

Sharp and Deadly

Getting stuck by a porcupine's quills is very painful.

The quills are hard to remove because each one has tiny hooks on its tip that stick in the enemy's skin.

Heat and moisture from an enemy's body draw the sharp quills deeper inside.

Sometimes a quill goes so deep that it hits a lung or heart.

When this happens, the enemy dies.

quills

When a porcupine falls, it sometimes stabs itself with its own quills. Yet this is no problem for the prickly creature. All porcupines learn how to use their sharp **claws** and teeth to yank out quills.

Tiny Pincushions

All porcupines are born with a full set of quills.

At first the tiny quills are soft, but they harden an hour or two after birth.

The baby, called a porcupette, weighs about as much as two oranges.

It can see and hear, and has several small teeth.

A mother porcupine gives birth in a **den**. This home might be in a cave, a hollow log, or under a pile of rocks.

Tree Houses

Porcupines sleep during the day and are awake at night.

They do most of their sleeping in tall trees.

The sharp claws and the bumpy pads on their paws help them climb.

Until a porcupette learns to climb a tree, it sleeps in a den with its mother.

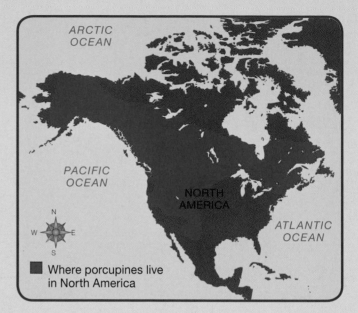

ARCTIC OCEAN

PACIFIC OCEAN

NORTH AMERICA

ATLANTIC OCEAN

N W E S

■ Where porcupines live in North America

Different types of porcupines are found all over the world, except in Australia and Antarctica. Porcupines in North America live mostly in forests.

Tasty Trees

Not only do porcupines sleep in trees, they eat them, too.

These prickly creatures eat tree leaves, branches, and fruit.

In winter, they use their long orange teeth to bite off tough **bark**.

Porcupines also chew on grass, clover, and other plants.

bark

Porcupines usually won't eat from the trees that they live in. After sleeping all day, porcupines climb down from their tree houses to look for food in different trees.

Living and Learning

Each night the prickly porcupette follows its mother as she looks for tasty meals.

When the mother climbs a tree, she grunts for her baby to follow.

She also leads her young to water to practice swimming.

Its quills help keep it afloat.

Porcupines are ready to leave their mothers when they are about six months old.

A Long, Prickly Life

A porcupine can live up to ten years in the wild.

During this time it meets many enemies.

Most enemies know not to mess with the prickly porcupine.

Other enemies have to learn the hard way.

Ouch!

fisher

The fisher is one enemy that has found a way to outsmart the porcupine. It bites the porcupine on its nose several times and flips it over. Then the fisher attacks the porcupine's soft belly, which has no quills.

Another Prickly Defense

Porcupines aren't the only animals with a prickly way of defending themselves. The hedgehog has about 7,000 sharp spines that cover most of its body. When in danger, a hedgehog rolls its body into a tight ball so that only its spines show. Only a few enemies are brave enough to approach this prickly pincushion.

Glossary

bark (BARK)
the tough covering on the outside of a tree

claws (KLAWZ)
sharp nails at the tip of an animal's fingers or toes

den (DEN)
a home where animals can rest, hide from enemies, and have babies

quills (KWILZ)
hard, sharp hairs that make up part of a porcupine's coat

Index

claws 10, 14

climbing 4, 14, 18

dens 12, 14

enemies 4, 6–7, 8, 10, 20, 22

fishers 20

food 4, 16, 18

hedgehogs 22

life span 20

porcupettes 12–13, 14, 18

quills 4–5, 6, 8, 10–11, 12, 18, 20

swimming 18

tails 4, 8–9

teeth 6, 10, 12, 16

trees 4, 14, 16, 18

Read More

Lang, Aubrey. *Baby Porcupine*. Ontario, Canada: Fitzhenry & Whiteside (2005).

Swanson, Diane. *Welcome to the World of Porcupines*. Vancouver, Canada: Whitecap Books (1999).

Zemlicka, Shannon. *Prickly Porcupines*. Minneapolis, MN: Lerner Publications (2003).

Learn More Online

To learn more about porcupines, visit
www.bearportpublishing.com/GrossOutDefenses

About the Author

Catherine Nichols has written many books for children, including several on animals. She lives in upstate New York with her dog and two cats.